HILARIOUS HOWLERS AND NUTTY NEWS

HILARIOUS HOWLERS AND NUTTY NEWS

Janet Rogers

Illustrated by Pete Beard

BEAVER BOOKS

A Beaver Book
Published by Arrow Books Limited
62–5 Chandos Place, London WC2N 4NW

An imprint of Century Hutchinson Ltd

London Melbourne Sydney Auckland
Johannesburg and agencies throughout the world

First published 1988

Set in Century Schoolbook
by JH Graphics Ltd, Reading

Made and printed in Great Britain
by Anchor Brendon Ltd
Tiptree, Essex

ISBN 0 09 958240 6

Contents

Introduction

I first started collecting funny newspaper misprints and all kinds of crazy howlers about five years ago when I spotted a headline in an East Sussex newspaper. The story beneath it wasn't very exciting but the headline caught my eye:

BODY IN GARDEN WAS A PLANT, SAID WIFE

Since then I've collected hundreds more and I have put all my favourites into this book. Every one of the Hilarious Howlers you will find in the pages that follow is real. It is either something somebody said or something that a newspaper or a magazine printed or it is a sign that has actually been spotted somewhere. I came across my own favourite silly sign only a few weeks ago when I visited a multi-storey office block in London and went to use the loo. There was a big notice hanging above the washbasins that said:

TOILETS OUT OF ORDER – PLEASE USE THE FLOOR BELOW

I *think* I know what they meant!

Some of the most hilarious howlers and most magnificent misprints come from abroad, and I am very grateful to my globetrotting friends who always try to add to my collection. While travelling in distant Nepal two of them discovered this gem in a Katmandu paper:

THOUGHT FOR TODAY
The whle wrod is in state of chassis

And from a New Zealand paper they brought me the news that:

NEW EXAMS TO BE INTRODUCED FOR SHEEP

Clearly they have well-educated lambs down under.

Everything in this book is for real – except for the three chapters of Nutty News Flashes that you will find at the beginning, in the middle and at the end. These are simply silly news items that my friends and I have invented. You might like to invent some more of your own. Have fun!

JR

And here is the Nutty News

A truckload of dogs was stolen this morning. Police looked for a lead and arrested a man at lunchtime, but they later released him. 'We were barking up the wrong tree,' said a police spokesman.

A woman was raced to hospital yesterday after she swallowed a bottle of toilet cleaner. The doctor who is treating her said, 'She has gone clean round the bend.'

In Swindon this morning two elephants were thrown out of the local swimming pool because they had only one pair of trunks between them.

The world's largest match factory has burned down. It happened when the workers went on strike.

Yesterday a Frenchman tried to commit suicide in Paris by jumping in the river. He was later declared to be in Seine.

A lorry carrying frogs has crashed on the M4. Police are hopping mad.

Harrogate dustmen have gone on strike for shorter hours. They say that sixty minutes is too long for an hour.

We've just heard from the Old Bailey that a man who stole a calendar has been sentenced to twelve months in gaol.

A lorry carrying cutlery has crashed on the south-bound carriageway of the A10. The police advise drivers to seek an alternative route as there are now too many forks in the road.

Job news. The Blotto Blotting Paper Company has announced that they have ten new job vacancies for young people who enjoy absorbing work.

Prince Edward had a surprise this morning when a young lady kissed him and he turned into a frog.

A set of traffic lights has been stolen in Macclesfield. The police say, 'Some people will stop at nothing.'

The famous scientist Professor Nutter has announced that Wales is sinking into the sea because of all the leeks in the ground.

Nottinghamshire farmers are meeting today to discuss the deaths of thousands of free-range chickens. A spokesman said that foul play was not suspected.

A taxi driver from Lincoln found a big box of kippers in his cab last night and took them to the police station. The police told him that if no one had claimed them in six months they would be his.

It was announced last night that there will be no more doughnuts on sale in Britain. The major manufacturer has decided to retire, saying that he is tired of the hole business.

News has just come in from Scotland that a Highland dancing display has had to be cancelled. The dancers washed their kilts and now they can't do a fling with them.

Police have caught a thief who has been stealing knickers from shops in Canterbury. 'It was a brief enquiry,' said a spokesman.

Flight 999 from Gatwick Airport had to be cancelled this morning due to wind. The captain apologized to passengers and said that he hoped his tummy would be better in time for tomorrow's flight.

Two ships have collided in the English Channel. One was carrying a cargo of red paint and the other was carrying blue paint. The crew are said to be marooned.

Early today a lorry carrying treacle crashed with a van full of meringues on the M1. Police are warning drivers to stick to their lanes.

Professor Nutter has invented a new cure for people who suffer from water on the knee. It's a tap on the leg.

Thieves have broken into a prune factory in the Midlands. Police say they're looking for men on the run.

The Pass First Time Driving School has announced that it's offering a free crash course to all new drivers.

Penzance Job Centre has announced vacancies for rubbish collectors in the town. No experience is needed for the job — you just pick it up as you go along.

Police are warning residents of Aberdeen to be on the look-out for a man who goes around puncturing aerosol cans. 'We don't know who he is but we suspect he is under extreme pressure,' said a spokesman.

A lorry load of soap was stolen from outside a supermarket in Hereford yesterday. The police say that the thieves made a clean getaway.

A lorry has just shed a load of lemons on the motorway. Police say they will have it cleared up in a Jif.

A frustrated artist collapsed at his home in Brighton today because he couldn't draw his breath.

A lorry carrying eggs, ham and mushrooms has crashed on the outskirts of Gloucester and created a giant omelette. Motorists travelling in the area are advised to carry their own knives and forks.

We have just heard that the marriage of the lighthouse keepers at Land's End is reported to be on the rocks.

A Sussex farmer who grows wheat, barley and oats has just sold his life story to a Sunday newspaper for cerealisation.

British Rail reported today that their new extra-fast passenger train had gone missing. A spokesman for the search team said they had nothing to go on but they were getting there.

Residents of a Cardiff suburb have complained that a thief is stealing their gates. However, they refuse to take the problem to the police in case the thief takes a fence.

A young man who wandered into a syrup factory and fell into a vat of treacle is reported to have come to a sticky end.

A thief who raided a camping site last week has been charged with robbery within tent.

Adam has announced that he intends to divorce Eve after she boiled his best suit and served it with roast beef for dinner.

Because of the strike by Derby gravediggers, all graves in the area will be dug by a skeleton staff.

All the light bulbs have been stolen from York public library. Librarians say that they are looking for someone who can shed light on the problem.

The winner of the Chef of the Year competition has been named. He is Roland Butter from Bridlington.

The case of the thief who held up three old-age pensioners and stole their false teeth has baffled police, but they say they're chewing it over.

The Meat Marketing Board announced yesterday that plans to wrap all its meat pies in tin had been foiled.

To combat the increasing crime rate architects have designed a new range of burglar-proof houses. They will be know as Sure Lock Holmes.

A hole has been found in the fence surrounding Sunnydale nudist camp. Police say they're looking into it.

British Telecom have announced this morning that they do not intend to make telephone poles any longer. Their press spokesman said that in their opinion they are quite long enough already.

An elderly lady who last month dialled 666 instead of 999 was surprised when today an Australian policeman turned up to answer the emergency.

A jeweller's shop was broken into last night and all the clocks and watches stolen. Police say that only time will tell.

The Irish intelligence agency has just cracked the Green Cross Code, but they promise to have it mended as soon as possible.

Police who are searching for thieves who stole fifty sets of snooker balls say that so far they haven't had a good break.

Ten gallons of Super Glue were stolen on Wednesday. Police say they are stuck for clues.

It was announced today that the headquarters of the Umpires Association was being transferred to the Umpire State Building in New York.

A television repair shop was burgled during the night and thieves got away with two hundred TV sets. Police say that all channels are being watched.

A chemist's shop has been robbed and the thieves got away with a number of bottles of perfume. Police say their tracker dogs are on the scent.

Mr Brisket the butcher has had all his meat stolen. The police say that he is very cut up about it.

A ton of human hair destined for the wig factory has been stolen. Police are combing the area.

A lorry full of snails has disappeared on its journey from Glasgow to Southampton. Police say they are following the trail.

Sid Brick, whose one-man bus crashed into a bridge in Birmingham yesterday, has told police that he has no idea how the accident happened as he was upstairs collecting fares at the time.

Hunters have reported that they have just shot the last white-tailed South African antelope in the world. So that is the end of the gnus.

Silly Signs

All these silly signs are real. They've been spotted in shop windows, on noticeboards, stuck on walls and in all sorts of places. Next time you're out for a walk, have a look round for more to add to this crazy collection!

Outside a jeweller's shop:
    EARS PIERCED WHILE YOU WAIT

Outside an electrical store:
    WHY GO ELSEWHERE TO BE CHEATED
    WHEN YOU CAN COME IN HERE!

Sign in a launderette:
    AUTOMATIC WASHING MACHINES:
    PLEASE REMOVE ALL YOUR CLOTHES
    WHEN THE LIGHT GOES OUT

In a dress shop window:
>DON'T STAND OUTSIDE AND FAINT –
>COME IN AND HAVE A FIT

Sign in a London department store:
>BARGAIN BASEMENT UPSTAIRS

In an office:
>WOULD THE PERSON WHO TOOK THE
>STEP LADDER YESTERDAY PLEASE BRING
>IT BACK OR FURTHER STEPS WILL BE
>TAKEN

Outside a farm:
>HORSE MANURE 50p PER PRE-PACKED BAG
>20p DO-IT-YOURSELF

In the window of a dry cleaner's:
>SAME DAY DRY CLEANING – ALL
>GARMENTS READY IN 48 HOURS

Road sign:
>TURN RIGHT FOR THE FAIRY GLEN.
>BEWARE HEAVY LORRIES

At the zoo:
PLEASE DO NOT FEED THE ELEPHANTS. IF YOU HAVE ANY PEANUTS OR BUNS PLEASE GIVE THEM TO THE KEEPER ON DUTY

In an office:
AFTER THE TEABREAK STAFF SHOULD EMPTY THE TEAPOT AND STAND UPSIDE DOWN ON THE DRAINING BOARD

On a church door:
'THIS IS THE GATE OF HEAVEN. ENTER YE ALL BY THIS DOOR.'
(THIS DOOR IS KEPT LOCKED BECAUSE OF THE DRAUGHT. PLEASE USE THE SIDE DOOR)

Outside a furniture shop:
OUR MOTTO: WE PROMISE YOU THE LOWEST PRICES AND WORKMANSHIP

Sign in a German café:
MOTHERS, PLEASE WASH YOUR HANS BEFORE EATING

Outside a secondhand shop:
   WE EXCHANGE ANYTHING – BICYCLES,
  WASHING MACHINES, ETC. WHY NOT
  BRING YOUR WIFE ALONG AND GET A
          WONDERFUL BARGAIN?

In a grocery shop:
   TRY OUR LOCAL BUTTER. NOBODY CAN
              TOUCH IT

In a Chinese restaurant:
  IF YOU ARE SATISFACTORY PLEASE TELL
        YOUR FRIENDS. IF YOU ARE NOT
  SATISFACTORY PLEASE TELL THE WAITER

Outside a farm:
        CATTLE PLEASE CLOSE GATE

Sign outside a new town hall which was to be opened
by the Prince of Wales:
      THE TOWN HALL IS CLOSED UNTIL
  OPENING. IT WILL REMAIN CLOSED AFTER
    BEING OPENED. OPEN TOMORROW

Outside a photographer's studio:
OUT TO LUNCH: IF NOT BACK BY FIVE, OUT
FOR DINNER ALSO

Sign on a farm gate:
DOGS FOUND WORRYING WILL BE SHOT

In a restaurant:
CUSTOMERS WHO FIND OUR WAITING
STAFF RUDE SHOULD SEE THE
MANAGERESS

Seen at the side of a Sussex road:
SLOW CATTLE CROSSING. NO
OVERTAKING FOR THE NEXT 100 YRS.

Outside a smart shop:
NO CHILDREN ALOUD

Seen outside a travel agent:
WHY DON'T YOU GO AWAY?

Notice in a pet shop:
BIRDS GOING CHEEP!

Outside a disco:
SMARTS IS THE MOST EXCLUSIVE DISCO
IN TOWN. EVERYONE WELCOME

Sign in a picture shop:
LET US PUT YOU IN THE PICTURE AND
FRAME YOU

In an electrical shop:
WHY SMASH YOUR PLATES WASHING UP?
LET ONE OF OUR DISHWASHERS DO IT
FOR YOU

Sign at a garden fete:
BABY SHOW. ALL ENTRIES TO BE HANDED
IN AT THE GATE

In a café window:
WAITRESSES REQUIRED FOR BREAKFAST

Found in a butcher's shop:
THESE SCALES ARE ACCURATE
NO TWO WEIGHS ABOUT IT!

Seen in a shop selling calculators and computers:
YOU CAN ALWAYS COUNT ON US

Notice in a restaurant:
OUR CUTLERY IS NOT MEDICINE SO
PLEASE DO NOT TAKE IT AFTER MEALS

Seen in an American department store at Christmas:
VISIT SANTA'S GROTTO. NO QUEUEING –
WE'RE THE ONLY STORE IN NEW YORK
WITH THREE SANTAS

Seen at an American undertaker's:
OSCAR'S FUNERAL PARLOR – WHERE
YOU'LL ALWAYS FIND A SMILE

Notice in a London park:
NO WALKING, SITTING OR PLAYING ON
THE GRASS IN THIS PLEASURE PARK

Seen in a Coventry factory:
ANY MEMBER OF STAFF WHO NEEDS TO
TAKE THE DAY OFF TO GO TO A FUNERAL
MUST WARN THE FOREMAN ON THE
MORNING OF THE MATCH

Sign warning of quicksand:
QUICKSAND. ANY PERSON PASSING THIS
POINT WILL BE DROWNED. BY ORDER OF
THE DISTRICT COUNCIL

Spotted outside a church:
DON'T LET STRESS AND WORRY KILL YOU
OFF – LET THE CHURCH HELP

Notice sent to residents of a Wiltshire parish:
DUE TO INCREASING PROBLEMS WITH
LITTER LOUTS AND VANDALS WE MUST
ASK ANYONE WITH RELATIVES BURIED IN
THE GRAVEYARD TO DO THEIR BEST TO
KEEP THEM IN ORDER

Sign in a chemist's shop:
>WE DISPENSE WITH ACCURACY

Spotted in a garden centre:
>UP THESE STEPS FOR THE SUNKEN
>GARDEN

Sign on a newly painted bench:
>WET PAINT. WATCH IT OR WEAR IT

Seen in a watch shop:
>PLEASE WAIT PATIENTLY TO BE SERVED.
>I ONLY HAVE TWO HANDS

Notice in the window of a shop selling fabrics:
>REPAIRS AND ALTERATIONS DONE HERE.
>DYING ARRANGED

Road sign:
>STEEPLE BUMSTEAD: LEFT 3 MILES
>RIGHT 3 MILES
>STRAIGHT
>AHEAD 3 MILES

Sign outside pet shop:
>NO DOGS ALLOWED

Notice in a dry cleaner's window:
ANYONE LEAVING THEIR GARMENTS
HERE FOR MORE THAN 30 DAYS WILL BE
DISPOSED OF

Spotted in a Blackpool guest house:
  HOT AND COLD RUNNING IN ALL ROOMS

Notice in Keighley restaurant:
  FROM MONDAY OUR CATERING
ASSISTANTS WILL BE PLEASED TO SERVE
  CUSTOMERS TO THE VEGETABLES

Seen outside a fire station:
  FIRE STATION – NO SMOKING

Notice on Norfolk village shop:
  HALF-DAY CLOSING ALL DAY
  WEDNESDAY

Sign in London pizza parlour:
  OPEN 24 HOURS – EXCEPT 2 A.M.–8 A.M.

Seen outside dancing academy:
  PLEASE MIND THE STEP

Sign in motorway garage:
  PLEASE DO NOT SMOKE NEAR OUR
PETROL PUMPS. YOUR LIFE MAY NOT BE
WORTH MUCH BUT OUR PETROL IS

Notice in health food shop window:
CLOSED DUE TO ILLNESS

Spotted in a safari park:
ELEPHANTS PLEASE STAY IN YOUR CAR

Circus poster:
BIFFO BROTHERS' CIRCUS, FEATURING
MARVO, THE STRONGEST MAN IN THE
WORLD. IN TOWN ALL WEAK

Sign outside a church in Hemel Hempstead:
THE LAST WORLD WAR. WHERE AND
WHEN WILL IT BE FOUGHT? ST
MARGARET'S, HARTFORD STREET ON
TUESDAY 22ND FEBRUARY AT 7.00 P.M.

Seen during a conference:
FOR ANYONE WHO HAS CHILDREN AND
DOESN'T KNOW IT, THERE IS A CRÈCHE
ON THE FIRST FLOOR

Sign in a tea shop:
TODAY'S SPECIAL. POT OF TEA WITH
STONES AND JAM, £1

Spotted in a golf club:
GOLFERS PLEASE DO NOT DRINK AND
DRIVE

Seen in a college:
THIS WEEK'S LECTURE: UNDERWATER
LIFE BY PETER FISH

Notice in hairdresser's window:
STYLIST WANTED. GOOD PAY AND
FRINGE BENEFITS

Notice in a field:
THE FARMER ALLOWS WALKERS TO
CROSS THE FIELD FOR FREE, BUT THE
BULL CHARGES

Sign at the tennis club:
WOULD SPECTATORS PLEASE BE QUIET
DURING MATCHES AND LET THE PLAYERS
RAISE A RACQUET

Spotted at the railway station:
PASSENGERS ARE ASKED NOT TO CROSS
THE LINES – IT TAKES AGES FOR US TO
UNCROSS THEM AGAIN

Notice at the zoo:
CHILDREN FOUND STRAYING WILL BE
SENT TO THE LION ENCLOSURE

Message on a leaflet:
IF YOU CANNOT READ, THIS LEAFLET WILL
TELL YOU HOW YOU CAN GET LESSONS

Sign on repair shop door:
WE CAN REPAIR ANYTHING. (PLEASE
KNOCK HARD ON THE DOOR – THE BELL
DOESN'T WORK)

Sign in office block, pinned to escalator:
LIFT OUT OF ORDER. PLEASE USE
ELEVATOR

Traffic sign:
PARKING RESTRICTED TO 60 MINUTES IN
ANY HOUR

Sign at Norfolk farm gate:
BEWARE! I SHOOT EVERY TENTH
TRESPASSER AND THE NINTH ONE HAS
JUST LEFT

Notice in church hall:
ELECTRICAL SPECIALIST WILL BE HERE
ON THURSDAY MORNING TO SHOW
PARISHIONERS HOW TO WIRE PLUGS AND
MAKE SMALL REPAIRS. FOLLOWED BY A
LIGHT LUNCH

Sign spotted in farmyard:
MANURE FOR SALE. BRING YOUR OWN
BUCKET

Spotted in a toilet in a London office block:
TOILET OUT OF ORDER. PLEASE USE
FLOOR BELOW

Terrible Translations

If English speakers have so much trouble with their own language, is it any wonder that foreigners come up with some absolutely terrible translations? Here are some examples of English abroad.

During a conference a Russian interpreter tried to cope with the phrase 'out of sight, out of mind'. When at a later date it was translated back into English it was discovered that it had been interpreted as 'invisible lunatic'!

Spotted in a guide book to an Italian museum: Attention must draw to a collection of local beetles – modestly encased in drawers, but one wonders at the exhibition.

From a Maltese guide book:
Although every care has been taken, us do not accept responsibility for inoccuracies.

Sign in a Japanese hotel:
Sports jackets may be worn, but no trousers.

Traffic advice in Italy:
To relieve traffic digestion, take the Astorio ferry every fifteen minutes.

Sign in Swiss hotel:
Do you wish to change in Zurich? Do so at the hotel bank!

Notice in a Spanish hotel:
It is forbidden to steal hotel towels, please. If you are not person to do such is please not to read this notice.

Spotted at an Italian camp-site:
By order of the Police, one obliges the frequenters of the Camping to are wearing bath-costumes that are not giving offence to the Morals.

Notice in an Italian hotel:
Do not adjust your light hanger. If you wish more light see manager.

Notice in a Katmandu bus station:
The comfort of our buses is next to nun.

Cooking instructions taken from an Italian food packet:
Besmear a backing-pan, previously buttered with a good tomato sauce and after, dispose Canelloni, lightly distanced betweem them in a only couch.

Notice in an Austrian hotel:
In case of fire please do your utmost to alarm the hall porter.

Fire instruction in a French hotel:
In the event of fire the visitor, avoiding panic, is to walk down the corridor to warm the chambermaid.

Sign outside a French café:
Persons are requested not to occupy seats in this cafe without consuming.

Advert in a Spanish paper:
English shorthand typist. Efficien. Useless. Please apply . . .

Spotted at Belgian agency which forwarded luggage abroad:
Hand your baggage to us. We will send it in all directions.

Washing instructions with German socks:
The manufacturers of this hose must be washed in luke warm water, never hot and remove soap from water.

Instructions in a lift:
To move the cabin, push buttons of wishing floor. If the cabin shuld enter more persons, each-one should press number of wishing floor. Driving is then going alphabetically by natural order. Button retaining pressed position shows received command for visiting station.

Sign in Egyptian hotel:
If you require room servie please open door and shout 'Room service'.

Sign in Sorrento hotel:
Our concierge will be happy to supply you with stamps, postcards and any information you may require. We would ask you to contact the concierge immediately if you should have any problem regarding the hotel and its services. Please don't wait last minutes to report difficults. Then it will be too late to arrange any inconveniences.

Notice in an Italian hotel:
Visitors are requested not to throw coffee or other matter into the basin. Why else it stuffs the place inconvenient for the other world.

Belgian cafe menu:

Hand and eeg
Pissoles and reas
Frightened eeg
Sauceage eeg and chaps

Cream dognuts
Roast apple tart with source
Biscuit cease

Italian menu:

Hen soop
Fungus with garlic
Kink prawns

Liver with stuffed
Red Mallet
Biff stek
Bruined squids

French beas
French fried ships
Spineitch
Sprouts of Brussels

Label on packet of Italian violin strings:
Thanks to this type of metal straings, it has been possible to achieve both the switness of sound and the softness, to feel that, one can recall the bowel strings of the past, but this type far better than the latter owing to the promptness in emission and the ready and stable tuning.

Sign in Cairo hotel:
GEISHA NIGHT CLUB. At the 12th floor overlooking a magnificent, scintillating view of Cairo by night is the Geisha Night Club . . . Take the elevator and press the 12th bottom now!!

39

Awful Adverts

For connoisseurs of clangers the small ads section of the paper is far more fun than the news. Here are some of the best misprints and errors.

MEAT FOR YOUR DEEP FREEZE. We supply best Scotch beef from Wales.

LOST: Antique painting showing Adam and Eve in Market Shopping Centre last Tuesday night.

ALSATIAN DOG FOR SALE. Lovely one-year-old dog. Eats anything, especially fond of small children.

WANTED FOR EVENING WORK. Male waitresses for local restaurant.

FOR SALE: Doctor's tent and camping gear. Doctor no further use.

Beautiful country cottage for sale. 2 bedrooms, lounge, dining-room, fitted kitchen, bathroom, separate toilet 7 miles from Stratford-on-Avon.

FOR SALE: 1981 Ford Escort. Red. One lady owner. All reasonable offers rejected.

Young lady wants washing and cleaning three days a week.

DON'T MISS THE PUDDLEBY PLAYERS' PRODUCTION OF SOUTH PACIFIC! Another performance of this wonderful musical will be given on Saturday at 7 p.m. in the church hall. If you missed seeing it last week this will give you another chance to do so.

FOR SALE: Wedding dress, size 14, worn only twice.

WANTED: Mattress for gentleman stuffed with feathers.

EXPLOSIVES EXPERT REQUIRED. We need someone who can handle dynamite and who is prepared to travel unexpectedly.

SILVER LOCKET FOR SALE. Lovely heart-shaped locket on chain. Opens to allow insertion of two photographers.

DECORATOR. Need your house decorating? I specialise in inferior work!

SOFA FOR SALE: covered in yellow mustard.

Flat wanted for lady with good view and gas stove.

PIANO FOR SALE. Would suit learner with green legs.

LOVELY FARM COTTAGE FOR RENT. Sleeps 4 cows, sheep, lambs etc.

New widows made to order by experienced carpenter.

ANTIQUE TABLE. For sale, owned by elderly lady with wonderful carved legs.

INFLATABLE DINGHY FOR SALE. Good condition expect for puncture. £25.

HOLIDAY HOTEL. West Cornwall, beautiful views from lawns weeping down to sea.

FOR SALE: Two-bra electric fire, good condition.

LOST. Black and white female car called Puss. Reward offered for return.

STRADIVARIUS VIOLIN for sale. Almost new.

JOB VACANCY: Girl wanted for office manager.

WANTED. A qualified carpenter experienced in making antiques.

WANTED. Cooker, gas or electric, for young lady with brown enamel sides.

SINGLE LADY (35) non-smoker, does not drive, seeks same for motoring holiday in Wales.

FOR SALE. Brown pram with hood. 1.6L, five gears, capable of more than 100 m.p.h.

FOR SALE: An absolutely perfect lady's bicycle.

WEEKEND COTTAGE. Lovely weekend cottage, sleeps 4, fully equipped. Available Monday–Friday.

FOAM CUSHIONS. Brighten up your sofa and chairs with new foam rubber cushions at rock bottom prices.

FOR SALE. Genuine imitation leather sofa with genuine imitation mahogany arms.

CAR FOR SALE. Beautifully looked after by lady with no rust and a soft top.

RINGS BY POST. You can order our superb rings by post. To estimate size, tie a piece of string around your finger and send it to us.

MOBILE HOLE FOR SALE. Fully furnished, good condition.

WANTED. Reliable young lady to cook, wash and iron and milk a cow.

SIX MILLION DOLLAR MAN. £5 only.

TYPIST WANTED. Must speak proper and have floorless spelling.

COME FOR SUNDAY LUNCH AT HARVEY'S RESTAURANT – where good food is an unexpected pleasure.

FOR SALE: Delicate china statuette. Victorian. Belongs to lady slightly cracked.

FOR SALE. Electric guitar with amplifier. Very loud. Please write to: 24 Bull Lane, Puddleby.

FOR SALE. Two sets of ear plugs. Apply to: 26 Bull Lane, Puddleby.

WANTED: Complete drum kit with cymbals. Write to: 24 Bull Lane, Puddleby.

FOR SALE. Terraced house, 3 bedrooms, lounge, kitchen, bathroom, garage, gardens. Good price for quick sale. Apply: 26 Bull Lane, Puddleby.

SECRETARY REQUIRED. Shorthand typing essential but not absolutely necessary.

FLAT FOR RENT. 2 rooms, bathroom and kitchen. £40 a week including gas, electricity and rats.

RUBBISH CLEARANCE: satisfaction guaranteed or twice your rubbish back.

FOR SALE: Two office desks and two secretary's hairs.

WE DO ALL PRINTING JOBS BEST. There are no printing jobs no printing jobs, no printing jobs, no printing jobs that cannot be executed, cannot be executed more efficiently than by us.

SAME-DAY LAUNDRY. Leave your clothes with us and go and have a good time.

GET YOUR MILKMAN TO LAY SOME EGGS FOR YOU – ON YOUR DOORSTEP

LUXURY HONEYMOON COTTAGE. Sleeps three.

URGENTLY REQUIRED. Single-handed chef for small hotel.

FOR SALE. Ten-speed racing bike. Good condition. No wheels.

PUDDLEBY AMATEUR DRAMATIC SOCIETY. Auditions now being held for Christmas pantomime production of *Snow White and the Seven Dwarfs*. Only small parts left.

WEDDING RECEPTION? We can supply garden sheds, greenhouses and coal bunkers.

JOB OPPORTUNITY for salesman with at least 2 years' sales experience in the last 6 months.

JOE'S CAFÉ. We're famous for our tea and cakes and our tongue sandwiches speak for themselves!

NORFOLK BROADS. Charming holiday chalet only yards from the water. Reasonable germs.

ANTIQUES EXPERT offers rare eighteenth-century mahogany Chip & Dale dining-room set. Complete with telephone table and cocktail cabinet with space for video.

WANTED. Young man or woman to walk dog who doesn't smoke.

DRIVING SCHOOL. Always places for new pupils due to asses every week.

KILLIT PEST SPRAY. Kills all known household pets.

BABY BOILER. Good condition.

FOR SALE. Pushchair for twins. Babies of no further use.

HUNTSMEN. If you shoot yourself and have not used Popper's ammunition you have missed one of the pleasures in life.

WE MOVE PIANOS! If you need your piano moving call us. We've got years of experience. Call: 222 4567

FIREWOOD FOR SALE. Bundles of good quality firewood. We will deliver. Phone: 222 4567.

MAN WITH CHAINSAW requires apprentice to lend him a hand.

BOAT FOR SALE: Motor cruiser. Colour: white vanished.

FOR SALE: Set of tools complete with wench.

HOUSE FOR SALE. Sexi-detached with four bedrooms.

DRIVING LESSONS. We have the latest models. Learn to drive while you watch TV!

WESTWOOD WINES: If it's quality wine you want, try us — the best is none too good.

EXPERIENCED LADY seeks job as housekeeper. Likes cleaning and cooing.

ONE collapsible baby, excellent condition, £45.

WANTED: A man to stick on tiles.

PEKING PARLOUR: Visit the best Chinese restaurant in town. We serve all types of Chinese chefs!

BELGIAN/GERMAN/SWISS chef required for famous French restaurant.

PUPPY FOR SALE. Labrador puppy, 3ft by 6ft 6ins, blue and white striped mattress.

FOR SALE: Two mathematical rabbits. Will multiply quickly.

JOBS! JOBS! JOBS! We need four technicians to work in our high-tech lasertronic astro-research laboratory. No experience necessary.

WANTED: Model willing to pose for nude artist.

ONE-DAY DRY CLEANING. We do not tear your clothes with machinery. We do it carefully by hand.

HAIR RAISING. Visit our new Puddleby salon. Hair cut while you wait.

WANTED. Man to wash dishes and a waitress for new restaurant.

TO RENT. Two-bedroomed flat, central heating, bathroom near bus stop.

PEASANTS. Delicious fresh peasants for your special dinner party. From Burrows the Butcher.

JOB OPPORTUNITY. We have an unexpected vacancy for a knife-thrower's assistant. Please apply to Biffo Brothers' Circus.

FOR SALE: Food processor with all attachments including tooth extractor.

SENIOR CITIZEN REQUIRED for cleaning work, including hovering.

JOB WANTED. Unemployed lady seeks work. Completely reliable and honest, will take anything.

LOST: Small mongrel, black and white ears, tail and feet missing since last Tuesday.

FOR SALE. Genuine 100% nylon wigs. These wonderful wigs look totally natural. Colours: green, blue, orange, purple and scarlet.

BARGAIN HOLIDAYS. You can visit Australia for less than £10000000000000000000000000000000! Remarkable value!

ROMERO'S RESTAURANT wish to announce that they now serve Sunday lunches seven days a week.

FOR SALE: 2 nice dresses, 40″ bust, suit elderly lad.

WE'LL SHOOT YOUR CHILDREN FOR CHRISTMAS! Call Quick-Snap Photographic.

WANT TO GIVE UP SMOKING? Try our ant-smoking clinic, held every Wednesday at the health centre.

J.J. LEAKY AND SONS for Leaky boats, the best you can buy.

DATING AGENCY. Are you lonely? We have lots of fiends just waiting to meet you.

FREE RANGE EGGS. Try our fresh eggs – you can't beat them!

SMITH AND JONES, FUNERAL DIRECTORS. Parties catered for.

MORRIS MINOR FOR SALE. 1968, good condition. New engine. This will not last long.

ANTIQUE FURNITURE FOR SALE. Almost new!

PARKER'S SHOE SHOP. Come and see our new selection of summer vandals.

Come to the Country Lover's lecture in St Mary's Church Hall on Tuesday at 7 p.m.. The lecture will be entitled, 'Preserving our Wildlife'.

COME TO SAFEBURY'S for good food. This week's special offers: Hedgehog flavoured crisps and squirrel pie.

CROCODILE FOR SALE, or will swap for a wooden leg.

FINE RAT SALE. Come and buy yourself a beautiful painting at our exhibition in the Town Hall.

FLYING LESSONS. No crash courses given.

YOUNG MAN seeks doom in town centre, near to station and shops.

1936 HEARSE FOR SALE. Black, low mileage, with original body.

NEW WASHING MACHINES. All makes. Don't kill your wife – let our washing machines do the dirty work for you!

WANTED: Woman to run up curtains.

FOR SALE: Fish van, with scales, £1,200.

BOAT FOR SALE. One owner, green in colour.

WANTED: Domesticated lady to live with elderly gentleman to hell with the cooking and cleaning.

Youth wanted to train as petrol pump attendant. Elderly man would suit. Please call Puddleton 222444.

ERRORS. No responsibility can be accepted for losses arising from typographical errors. Advertisers are expected to check their own smalls to ensure 9qp0,8743xr1q93042yr . . . .sufcgn!.

Grave Errors

You might think that it would be easy to bury someone and inscribe a tribute on their headstone without making a mistake. Unfortunately, as you can see below, grave errors do happen!

This gallant young man
gave up his life
in the attempt
to save a perishing lady

To the memory of Anne-Louise
A local woman
1813–1857
Built by Charles Frodsham

Richard Kendrick
was buried August 29th, 1785
at the wish of his wife
Margaret

Erected to the memory of
JOHN PHILIPS
Accidentally shot
As a mark of respect by his brother

Underneath this pile of stones
Lie the remains of Mary Jones:
Her name was Lloyd, it was not Jones
But Jones was put to rhyme with stones.

Here lies Ann Mann;
She lived an old maid and
she died an old Mann

Here lies
John James Cook
who was a faithful servant to his master
and an upright downright honest man

Here lies Philip Archer
Gone to be an angle

To the memory of
Dorothy Cecil
Unmarried as yet

Erected to the memory of
John MacFarlane
Drowned in the waters of Leith
By a few affectionate friends

Sacred
to the memory of
Major James Brush
who was killed
by the accidental discharge
of a pistol by his orderly
14th April 1831
Well done thou good
And faithful servant

Here lies the body of John Eldred.
At least, he will when he is dead.
But now at this time he is alive
The 14th August, sixty-five.

Here lies
John Higley
whose father and mother were drowned
in the passage from America
Had they both lived
they would have been buried here.

Here lies the body of
Sarah
wife of John Hayes
who died 24th March 1823 AD
aged 42 years.
The Lord giveth and the Lord taketh away
Blessed be the name of the Lord.

Here lies the body of John Mound
Lost at sea and never found.

Alice Mary Johnson 1898
Let her RIP

Fake Facts

Everyone knows that bulls charge at things coloured red, don't they? And that Dick Whittington had a cat and that bagpipes were invented in Scotland. . . . Well, think again! All of these 'facts' are fakes — they are mistakes and myths that have passed into our general knowledge. If you're feeling strong enough to take the awful truth, read on!

Nothing could be more English than an umbrella, could it? Many people think that umbrellas are a British invention developed by the Victorians. In fact they were first used by the Chinese nearly 3,000 years ago! Chinese umbrellas were made of varnished paper on a bamboo frame and they were most often used as parasols, to protect people from the heat of the sun. The ancient Egyptians also had umbrellas, but they didn't reach Britain until about 1740, when a man called Jonas Hanway became the first person to carry one regularly against the rain.

What is the most common disease in the world? 'Flu? The common cold? No – it's tooth decay, which affects almost everyone in the world!

The Canary Islands must be named after the canary birds that are found there, surely? No, they're not! Originally they were known in Latin as the *Insulae Canariae*, which means 'Islands of the Dogs' because there were lots of dogs there. Later the name became written as Canary Islands, and the birds were named after the islands!

Great Dane dogs do not come from Denmark, as their name would seem to suggest, but from Germany where they were originally trained to trot beside the carriages of wealthy people and protect them from highway robbers.

Many people believe that you can only see rainbows during the day, but this is not true. Rainbows are caused by the refraction of rays of light on raindrops. If there is a shower of rain on a bright moonlit night, it's sometimes possible to see a 'moonbow'. If you're keen on rainbow-spotting, don't try looking for one at midday. At that time the sun is too high in the sky to create the effect.

Many people believe that bulls are roused to anger when they see something red in colour, hence the saying 'It's like a red rag to a bull'. Because of this belief matadors use a red cape to encourage the bull to charge at them during bullfights. But in fact bulls are almost completely colourblind and can't tell the difference between red and any other shade. Experts say that it is the swishing movement of the bullfighter's cape that irritates the animal and makes it charge. And they say that while bulls will charge a person wearing clothes, they ignore nudists because they think they are just naked animals like themselves. So if you ever find yourself in a field with a charging bull you know what to do — take off your clothes!

What do you think the black bit in the middle of your lead pencil is made of? The obvious answer is lead, but in fact there is no lead in modern lead pencils. The black bit in the middle of modern pencils is made of graphite. This is good news for all those people who suck the ends of their pencils, because lead is poisonous!

If you are a pantomime fan it's quite likely that you will have been to see *Dick Whittington*. And even if you haven't, you probably know the story about how Dick came to London to make his fortune and brought with him his cat. It's a lovely story, but sadly, it's not all true! Richard Whittington was born around the year 1358 in Gloucestershire. He came to London and made his fortune as a mercer, importing and selling fabrics such as silk and linen, and became famous throughout the city. He must have been respected too, because he was elected Lord Mayor of London three times, in the years 1397, 1406 and 1419. So the saying 'Turn again Dick Whittington, thrice Lord Mayor of London' is actually true. In 1605 someone wrote a popular play about him and invented the whole story of the cat. However, there was one real cat in his life. It didn't have four legs; it was his ship, *The Cat*, which used to carry all those silks and linens back to London!

The bald eagle is the symbol of the United States of America, but did you know that it is not really bald at all? It looks as if the top of its head is bald but in fact it is covered in flat white feathers.

What could be more Scottish than the bagpipes? Lots of things, actually, because the Scots didn't invent the bagpipes! They were first played in ancient Persia more than a thousand years ago, and in Egypt and Greece, too, before the Romans took them up. It was from them that the Scots got the idea and the bagpipes have since become the national instrument of Scotland. So next time you hear a noise like a dozen tom cats being strangled don't blame the Scots – blame the ancient Persians and the Romans! Continuing on the Scottish theme, although tartan is definitely Scottish in origin, the kilt isn't. The first kilts were worn in France and not north of the border!

White elephants are not white. They should correctly be called albinos because they suffer from the same condition that many humans suffer from – albinism. The problem is caused by a lack of coloured pigment in the hair, skin and eyes, which means that human albinos have white or pale blond hair, white skin and pale pink or blue eyes. Many species of animal and even plants suffer from the problem. In elephants the colour of the skin is not affected and they are the same grey as all other elephants. But if you look closely, you'll find that white elephants have pink eyes!

Do you play darts? As far as most people are concerned, darts is just a game invented to play in pubs and clubs. But that's wrong. Darts were originally invented hundreds of years ago as weapons! They were used in battle by archers.

When the enemy got too close for the archers to use their bows and arrows effectively they would pull out their darts and throw them at the opposition. Unfortunately we don't know what they scored for a bullseye. . . .

How did the turkey get its name? No, not because it comes from Turkey. In fact there are no turkeys in Turkey! The turkey is a member of the pheasant family and is native to America. There are two explanations about how it got its name. The first is that American settlers thought its profile looked like an outline of the map of Turkey. The second is that its cry sounds like the word 'turkey'. Take your pick!

If you've watched the *Jaws* series of films you can be forgiven for thinking that all sharks are killers. In fact of all the species throughout the world, fewer than ten have been known to attack man and only three can be said to be killers. None of the sharks which swim in British waters are dangerous and the largest of all, the whale shark, which reaches a length of 18m, eats nothing but marine plankton.

The world is round – we all know that. But we're all wrong, because the world is actually irregular in shape and only very roughly round. It bulges in the middle and it is flat at the top and bottom. And how about the North and South Poles? The North Pole is a fixed point, but not many people realize that the South Pole keeps moving as the world's magnetic fields shift. Every five years or so its new position is plotted, and sometimes it moves several kilometres!

The aubergine or eggplant is technically a fruit and not a vegetable. It's a member of the tomato family and, of course, everyone knows that a tomato is a fruit and not a vegetable – don't they?

The Battle of Hastings was not actually fought in Hastings. The English and French armies met in fields about 10km away and to commemorate the famous event the place was given a name – Battle.

Despite their name, centipedes do not have a hundred legs. They have two legs for every segment of their bodies; a long centipede might have fifty segments and one hundred legs, but most centipedes are much smaller.

Many people think that computers are very intelligent – more intelligent than human beings. However, despite their speed and efficiency at doing certain tasks, they are not in fact very clever. According to experts, the average IBM computer has about the same intelligence as a beetle.

According to the popular saying, lightning never strikes twice in the same place. But in fact it does! Many people have been struck by lightning more than once and one man, an American forest ranger, has been struck seven times.

Ancient Greek statues and temples are often praised for their classical simplicity; so are the interiors of our most ancient cathedrals and churches. What most people don't appreciate is that they were not always so plain and undecorated. Many Greek buildings and statues, and many British cathedrals, were once covered in gaudy painted designs!

Most people think of gorillas as being covered all over with thick hair but they are not. Their chests are completely bald. And they are not the ferocious beasts that one might think from films like *King Kong*. Unless they are attacked or threatened gorillas are extremely gentle and sociable animals.

Visitors to London often think that Big Ben is the name given to the clock tower at the Houses of Parliament, but it's not. Nor is it the name of the clock. Big Ben is in fact the name of the bell which hangs in the tower. It was made in 1858 and christened after Sir Benjamin Hall, the clerk of works who supervised its construction.

St Bernard dogs do not carry a small barrel of brandy around the neck to revive travellers lost in the snow. This myth arose after Sir Edwin Landseer brightened up a painting showing a dog rescuing a traveller by adding a red brandy barrel around the dog's neck. This picture made the dogs famous in Britain, and everyone who saw it thought that they really did carry barrels of brandy!

Instant coffee is thought by most people to be a modern time-saving invention, but in fact instant coffee has been available since the middle of the eighteenth century.

What kind of animal lays the largest eggs in the world? An ostrich, perhaps, or an alligator? No. The world's largest egg is laid by a shark!

A pineapple does not grow in a pine tree, nor is it an apple. It is technically a berry.

Halley's Comet must be named after the man who discovered it — that's a mistake that many people make. It's certainly true that the comet is named after Edmund Halley, the famous astronomer, but he did not discover it. It was first spotted by Chinese star-gazers hundreds of years earlier, but it was Halley who worked out that it circled the earth regularly and predicted that it would appear in 1759. He was right, and after its appearance on schedule it was named after him.

Turkish baths were not invented by the Turks but by the Romans.

A ten-gallon hat does not hold ten gallons of water. It holds about three-quarters of a gallon.

You might think that because of its long neck, a giraffe has many more vertebrae than a man. But in fact the giraffe has the same number as a man.

Everyone knows that rhubarb is a fruit – after all, you eat it with custard like other fruit! But in fact rhubarb is a vegetable.

If you have ever seen a famous television advert which shows chimpanzees doing all sorts of things, you may think that monkeys can smile, but you would be wrong. Man is the only creature who smiles. When monkeys bare their teeth and appear to smile, they are in fact displaying fear and aggression.

Surely there can't be many animals more dangerous than a roaring male lion? Actually there can – a lioness! Ninety per cent of the hunting and killing done by a pride of lions is done by the females. And by the way, according to experts the most dangerous of all the African game creatures is not the rhino, the elephant or the giraffe but the hippopotamus.

The koala bear is not actually a bear – it's a marsupial.

Which city has the most canals – Venice or Birmingham? Amazingly enough it's not Venice, famous for centuries for its romantic canals, but Birmingham!

If you were asked to guess the month in which hail was most common in Britain you would probably choose a winter month, when the weather is really cold. But in fact hail is most common in the summer, particularly in June.

Don't be fooled into thinking that Greenland is green – it isn't. It's an inhospitable place, covered in ice. It was named Greenland by Eric the Red, an ancient Norse leader from Iceland who wanted to encourage people to go there. Strangely enough, despite its name Iceland is much more green and mild than Greenland.

King Richard III has gone down in folklore as a wicked hunchback, but in fact historical evidence indicates that there has been a long campaign to blacken his name. Despite Shakespeare's description of him, it's unlikely that he was a hunchback and his behaviour wasn't much worse, or much better, than that of many others at the time. On the other hand, one of the most famous of all English kings is Richard I, known as the brave and romantic Richard the Lionheart. From the evidence it seems that his reputation is much better than he deserves. He spent only six months of his ten-year reign in England because most of the time he was off enjoying himself on his Crusades.

Queen Victoria was not actually christened Victoria. Her names were Alexandrina Victorina.

Saint George, the patron saint of England, certainly never came to England. What's more he's the patron saint of several other countries, including Greece.

Nutty News Flash!

We interrupt this book to bring you the latest Nutty News Flashes!

News Flash!
A new type of cheese has been developed in Sunderland. It will be called Two-Handed Cheese because you eat it with one hand and hold your nose with the other.

News Flash!
Two electric fire manufacturers were arrested for having a fight in the middle of Sheffield last night. One said, 'We were just having a heated argument.'

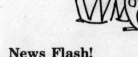

News Flash!
A man who was wrongly arrested and accused of burgling an optician's shop said, 'The police have made a right spectacle of themselves.'

News Flash!

A pint of milk and a tin of pilchards were stolen from a supermarket in Bristol this morning. Police say they suspect a cat burglar.

News Flash!
Professor Nutter and his assistants have just succeeded in crossing Concorde with a kangaroo and have come up with an aeroplane ideal for making short hops.

News Flash!
The Red Cross has announced that it will be recruiting cats next year. Asked why, a spokesman replied, 'We are in need of more Red Cross kits.'

News Flash!
A Chinese bank robber was caught as he made his getaway. He went up a one-way street – the wong way.

News Flash!
We have just received a newsflash from the United States. The president asks people throughout the world to stop sending telegrams and letters to Washington; he is dead.

News Flash!
Bird-lovers in Liverpool have reported the sighting of an owl that goes 'tweet tweet'. Apparently it doesn't give a hoot.

News Flash!
Buckingham Palace announced this morning that in future when Prince Harry burps the Queen will issue a royal pardon.

News Flash!
A lorry load of five-legged ladies' tights were stolen from Newcastle last night. Police are asking any ladies whose tights fit them like a glove to get in touch.

News Flash!
Two refuse vans were involved in a crash this morning. No one could decide who was to blame and one angry driver said, 'Allegations that the accident was my fault are a load of rubbish.'

News Flash!
A man who swallowed a barometer was raced to hospital last night. This morning doctors described his condition as 'Fair – but stormy later.'

News Flash!
A man was found dead in a cemetery this morning. A police spokesman said, 'This is a very grave case.'

News Flash!

A man arrested for walking through Coventry city centre wearing only a newspaper explained to the police yesterday that he always liked to dress with *The Times*.

News Flash!

A man from Bognor Regis has just been awarded the title of Laziest Man of the Year. To find out whether it was raining he used to call his dog in to see if it was wet.

News Flash!

Professor Nutter has invented a new cure for a runny nose. You just put your foot out and trip it up.

News Flash!

A woman from Miami is reported to have given birth to a foal. Doctors say her condition is stable.

News Flash!

A Conservative party spokesman has said there is no truth in the rumour that Mrs Thatcher is pregnant. It's only Labour pains.

News Flash!
News has come in from St Alban's that a man
stayed up all last night trying to work out what
happened to the sun when it went down. It finally
dawned on him.

News Flash!
A man was found guilty of sticking Green Shield
savings stamps on his insurance card yesterday.
He was given a six-month jail sentence and a set
of coffee mugs.

News Flash!
An American inventor has crossed a bag of flour
with a tin of baked beans and produced a cake that
blows out its own candles.

News Flash!
A report has just come in that an elephant has
done a ton on the M11. Police have warned
motorists to drive carefully and treat it as a
roundabout.

News Flash!
A tanker full of hair-remover has overturned on
the M21. Police say that it's a hair-raising clean-
up operation.

News Flash!
A man who broke into a cheese factory and stole
three tons of Cheddar confessed to police that he
was crackers.

News Flash!
A woman in Sussex who has spent the last six
months on a coconut diet says that she didn't lose
any weight but she's now really good at climbing
trees.

News Flash!

A boy in Rotherham has been hiccupping for two days. His teacher told him that he could stop himself by holding his breath and counting to a million.

News Flash!

Thieves broke into a shop and stole bottles of whisky, wigs and sweets. The police are now on the lookout for drunken bald-headed men with a sweet tooth.

News Flash!

A Dorset boy who spent all his time curled up underneath his bed has been examined by doctors. They have discovered that he thinks he is a little potty.

News Flash!

Police are investigating the theft of a toilet from the police station. 'At the moment we have nothing to go on,' said a detective.

News Flash!
Police have asked the motorist who took the second turning off the M3 last night to put it back.

News Flash!
Six men who broke into a paint factory were caught red, green, yellow, blue, orange and pink-handed.

News Flash!
A man in Newmarket has reported that his house has been burgled by a raving lunatic. When asked by police why he thought the burglar was mad the man replied, 'Because he left the video and TV and took my wife!'

News Flash!
A woman in Caernarfon phoned her travel agent yesterday and asked him how long it would take to fly to Australia. 'Just a minute,' said the travel agent, and the lady thanked him and hung up.

News Flash!
British Rail has announced cutbacks to its Paddington service. A spokesman for commuters said, 'Passengers will be hit by these cancelled trains.'

News Flash!
Staff from the local park have requested people not to take pots of tea on to the lawns. Their hot bottoms are killing the grass.

News Flash!
After consuming 200 sandwiches, 120 sausage rolls and 100 portions of jelly and ice-cream, Major Jump presented awards to all the boys who had won races at the school sports day.

News Flash!
The electricity company have warned that to touch their overhead power cables will cause instant death. Anyone found doing so will be prosecuted.

News Flash!
A thousand blunt pencils have been stolen from a factory in Lancaster. Police say that the crime seems pointless.

News Flash!
Following the theft of a sack of carrots and a packet of cigarettes from Sainsbury's police say they are looking for a rabbit with a cough.

News Flash!
The managing director of Sharp's Scissors has admitted that the firm has gone bankrupt after thousands of pairs of scissors were returned because they didn't work. 'We simply weren't good enough, to put it bluntly,' he said.

News Flash!
News has just come in of a race between a cabbage, a tap and a tomato. The cabbage was ahead, the tap kept running slowly, but in the end the tomato managed to ketchup.

News Flash!
A man has been arrested after driving his lorry on to Ascot racecourse, dumping a load of rubbish by the starting gate and setting light to it. He says it was his hot tip for the 4.30 race.

News Flash!
Mrs Hilda Parsons, who was tied to a refrigerator by a burglar who robbed her house, has been praised by police for her coolness.

Schoolbook Howlers

This is a collection of classic howlers taken from children's schoolbooks. Have you ever made any mistakes like these?

'The three wise men brought the baby Jesus Gold, Frankenstein and Myrrh.'

'Conservation is when you talk to people.'

'When a dog has puppies you call them a litre.'

'The Pope lives in the Vacuum.'

'Jacob is in the Bible and he has a brother called See-Saw.'

'Magnets are little creatures you find in rotten apples.'

'A surname is the name of somebody you say 'sir' to.'

'Moths don't eat anything except the holes in your clothes.'

'An oxygen has eight sides.'

'A vixen is what you call a lady vicar.'

'A blizzard is what you get inside a frozen chicken.'

'Newton discovered that when an apple gets ripe it falls to the ground.'

'I weigh five stone 4 inches.'

'A centimetre is an insect with 100 legs.'

'You find oysters in bed at the seaside.'

'A "shofar" is a man who drives a car for someone else.'

'The bride walked down the aisle carrying a big bunch of friesians.'

'Swallows live in people's stomachs.'

'Henry VIII had six wives and the second was Anne Berlin.'

'If you have something wrong with your feet you should go and see a pessimist.'

'Philatelists were a race of people who lived in Biblical times.'

'The Sewage Canal is in Egypt.'

'Herrings swim around the sea in shawls.'

'An executive is a man who used to chop people's heads off.'

'Nuclear power stations are built in places near the coast, such as Birmingham.'

'A vacuum is another name for a Hoover.'

'Income is a yearly tax that everyone has to pay.'

'When a man is married to just one woman it is called monotony.'

'People who test your eyes to see if you need glasses are called optimists.'

'Venison is a city in Italy with lots of canals.'

'The smallest wind instrument in an orchestra is called a Piccadilly.'

'A doggerel is a little dog.'

'The zodiac is in the sky. If you look closely you can see virgins, lions, crabs and goats at different months of the year.'

'A trombone is a musical instrument you play by pulling it in and out.'

'The radio was invented by Macaroni.'

'The earth resolves around the sun once every year.'

'Whales are hunted with large hairpins.'

'In France everyone drinks wine, even the pheasants.'

'The Bible of the Muslims is known as the Iran.'

'Poetry is a story when every line starts with a capital letter.'

'A, E, I, O and U are bowels.'

'The people who live in Paris are called Parisites.'

'A fjord is a Norwegian car.'

'Napoleon lost his naval at the Battle of Waterloo.'

'Shakespeare wrote tragedy, comedy and errors.'

'Henry VIII found it difficult to walk because he had an abbess on his knee.'

'The liver is one of the infernal organs.'

'Insects is what they burn in churches.'

'Shakespeare wrote *Henry IV* in two parts so that there would be room for the adverts in the middle.'

'Karl Marx was one of the Marx brothers. He played the harp.'

'There are lots of currants in the sea.'

'Soviet is another name for table napkins.'

'A civil serpent is a person who works for the government.'

'An autobiography is the history of motor cars.'

'Accoustic is what you use for hitting the ball in snooker.'

'My grandfather is retarded and lives on a pension.'

'Dust is the bits of fluff you find under your bed.'

'A reef is flowers you send to a funeral.'

'In the middle of Australia there is nothing at all.'

'An aperitif is a set of dentures.'

'The American flag is known as the Tarzan Stripes.'

'Depth is the same as height but upside down.'

'A widow is a wife with no man.'

'A criminal is someone who gets caught.'

'In a triangle, the square of the hippopotamus is equal.'

'In Africa people hunt rhinostriches.'

'Pineapples grow on pine trees.'

'A conservative is a glass porch on the side of a house.'

'People who live in Moscow are known as mosquitoes.'

'A skeleton is a man with his insides out and his outsides off.'

'The modern era is all the mistakes that are being made today.'

'When you play golf you have to wear a handy cap.'

'When a hippo has babies they are called hippies.'

'A refugee is the man who blows the whistle at football matches.'

'Noah had a wife who helped him with the animals. She was called Joan of Ark.'

'A compass tells you where to go and always points up the Pole.'

'Catholics believe what the Pope says but Protestants believe what they like.'

'A typhoon is a millionaire with a lot of money.'

'When the Queen was crowned she carried an orb and spectre.'

'Diplomacy means saying nasty things in a nice way.'

'Kangaroos keep their babies in their porches.'

'A hostage is a nice lady who serves drinks on aeroplanes.'

'Queen Elizabeth knitted Sir Walter Raleigh with a sword.'

'The Vikings were known as the Great Danes.'

'A lady's husband is called her spouse. If she has two husbands they are called her spice.'

'Doctors practise medicine until they get it right.'

'Tunisia and Amnesia are countries in north Africa.'

'Our cat has fleas so it keeps on etching.'

'Ratio was a sailor. His first name was Nelson.'

'Jewish priests are called rabbits.'

'The French national anthem is called the Mayonnaise.'

'Pot-pourri is a French dish served in little pots.'

Mr Goldwyn, Mr Spooner and Mrs Malaprop

Mr Samuel Goldwyn, the Reverend William Spooner and Mrs Malaprop are three people who have become famous throughout the world for their truly terrible howlers. So if you want your name to go down in history perhaps you'd better forget trying to get things right and concentrate on getting them wrong!

Mr Goldwyn

Samuel Goldwyn was a famous Hollywood film producer who came originally from Poland. He never quite got the hang of English and his famous slips of the tongue and muddled sayings have become famous as 'Goldwynisms'. Here are some of them.

A bachelor's life is no life for a single man.

Every director bites the hand that lays the golden egg.

A verbal contract isn't worth the paper it's written on.

Include me out.

In two words, im-possible!

I am willing to admit that I may not always be right, but I am never wrong.

If you can't give me your word of honour will you give me your promise?

I'll give you a definite maybe.

I had a great idea this morning but I didn't like it.

Talking about a plot for a film he once said, 'What we need is a story that starts with an earthquake and works its way up to a climax . . .'

Anyone who goes to a psychiatrist should have his head examined.

About one of his films he said, 'I don't care if it doesn't make a nickel. I just want every man, woman and child in America to see it!'

Someone suggested making a film about the life of Jesus and the twelve disciples. 'Why only twelve disciples?' asked Goldwyn. 'Go out and get thousands!'

Mr Spooner

The Reverend Spooner was Warden of New College at Oxford University from 1903 to 1924. He became famous for making slips of the tongue that were so funny they have become known as 'Spoonerisms'.

To a student who had missed his history lessons he said: 'You have hissed all my mystery lectures.'

To a lazy student: 'You have tasted a whole worm.'

After some bad news: 'I have just received a blushing crow.'

On a visit to the Dean: 'Is the bean dizzy?'

To a student who was being expelled: 'You will leave Oxford on the next town drain.'

When he sat in the wrong chair: 'I do apologize I am afraid I was sewn into this sheet.'

On his favourite form of transport: 'Give me a well-boiled icycle.'

Talking about a cat: 'I tried to stroke it, but it popped on its draws and ran out of the room.'

Raising his glass for a royal toast: 'Gentlemen, raise your glasses to the queer old dean.'

On finding his seat occupied in church: 'Excuse me, you are occupewing my pie.'

Commenting on the bad weather: 'It's roaring with pain outside.'

To a badly behaved student: 'You have been caught fighting a liar in the quadrangle.'

New Spoonerisms are being coined all the time. During a *Blue Peter* programme one of the presenters told the audience, ' . . . and next week we'll have a feature on blind dogs for the guide.'

Even the Queen has problems with Spoonerisms. During a speech in Australia in 1977 she referred to: 'The twenty-fifth reign of my year'!

Mrs Malaprop

Mrs Malaprop is a character who appears in a play called *The Rivals* by Sheridan. She has the habit of confusing words that sound like each other but have different meanings, and she has given her name to similar mistakes, which are known as 'Malapropisms.'

These are some of the original Malapropisms from *The Rivals*.

'He is the very pine-apple of politeness.' (Instead of, 'He is the very pinnacle of politeness.')

'Illiterate him, I say, quite from your memory.' (Instead of, 'Obliterate him, I say, quite from your memory.')

Here's a collection of some more mistakes and slips of the tongue, when the speakers said things they didn't mean to!

'Would you grill the cat while I feed the toast, please?'

'I've just read this book by Thomas Hardy. It's called *Tess of the Dormobiles*.'

'She had to have her leg cut off right down to the foot.'

'I think they should have waited until all the old people were dead before they replaced feet and inches with metres.'

'Our teacher got so angry he bit Ryan's head off.'

'I prefer bidets to sheets and blankets.'

'If you don't come back I won't let you go again.'

'If we're going to keep our heads above water we'll have to keep our ears to the ground and our noses to the grindstone.'

'My father communicates to work on the train each day.'

'All of this ice is frozen.'

'A horse's hand measures about four inches.'

'Your head looks just like my brother's behind.'

'After my husband died I buried myself in the garden.'

'This house is so damp we have mildred on the wall.'

'When I go to bed I count the trees on the wallpaper. I always sleep like a log.'

'Muslims go to say their prayers in a kiosk.'

'The volcano erupted and all this molten lager came running down!'

'He gave me a lift in his car. It's a red hunchback.'

'The rain was dripping off the roof like water.'

'The weather forecast said there was going to be fist and mog tomorrow.'

'After the operation he had a scarf on his tummy.'

'The time is twenty-half and a five minutes past six.'

'My granny wears a long-sleeved cardinal to keep her warm.'

'He was sentenced to two years in prison as a detergent to other people.'

'My dad buys his sandwiches with luncheon vultures.'

'My grandad's suffering from greenfly this summer.'

'During the last war my dad was evaporated to the country.'

'We've bought a stimulated leather three-piece suite.'

And here are some more modern examples of Malapropisms. Can you work out the word the speakers *should* have used? The answers are at the bottom of the page.

My mum uses massacre on her eyes.

My Dad works as a refuge collector.

In our history lesson we learned about the French resolution.

The doctor gave me a conscription for some ointment.

107

Misprint Madness

These mistakes have been spotted in newspapers and magazines all over the world. Some of them are misprints, some are howlers. See how many you can find in your local paper!

'The latest fashion is for trousers striped like a zebra in black, scarlet, green, yellow and mauve.'

'Beat the egg into the sugar and butter mixture, then sift in the flour and add milk and flavourings. Pour into cake tins and bake for 40 minutes. Funeral services will be held on Tuesday afternoon at 3.30 p.m.'

'Last year 15,823 people visited the museum, which was twice as many people as the year before when no attendance figures were kept.'

'By an unfortunate typographical error we were made to say last week that the retiring officer was a member of the defective branch of the police force. Of course this should have read, "The detective branch of the police farce."'

'The new bride is more than forty feet wide and replaces the old one which collapsed into the river last May.'

'Pauline Corbett, the well-known ballet dancer, was involved in a serious car crash last week. However, we are pleased to report that she was able to dance yesterday evening in four pieces.'

'Miss Carpenter is friendly and easy to talk to. . . . She has a fine, fair skin which, she admits ruefully, comes out in a mass of freckles at the first hint of sin.'

'The bride's going away outfit was an attractive pale pink dress with matching jacket with navy trim. Both are well known locally and play badminton for the county.'

'Unless teachers receive more pay they will resign and leave their pests . . .'

'WEATHER REPORT: Today a deep depression will mope its way across northern England.'

'Mrs Norris, who won a brace of pheasants, kindly gave her prize bark and this was auctioned to raise a further £5.50 for the fund.'

'Dusan Vlaco, from Yugoslavia, the second-longest surviving heart transplant patient, has died in Los Angeles. He received the transplant on September 18 1698.'

'If you ask five of your friends to name a vegetable you will usually find that nine out of ten will say the carrot.'

'After the fire two women were admitted to hospital suffering from mild buns.'

'Ice cream sellers expect huge sales in this heat-wave weather and have ordered large socks to supply the demand.'

'At the request of residents, running water and toilets are to be installed at the cemetery.'

'In a bitterly cold wind, the Queen, wearing a warm sage-green tweed coat with a beaver lamb collar and a green mitre-installation of turbo-alternators and boilers.'

'The Prime Minister announced today that her campaign had been a hug success.'

'Unemployment dropped slightly last week, although the number of people out of work increased.'

'We note with regret that Mrs Janet Heath is recovering from her recent car crash.'

'Winger Michael Johnson was named Man of the Match after the game in which he scored three goats on Saturday.'

'At the Women's Institute slide show the ladies included their husbands and children in their potluck supper.'

'Never throw away old chicken bones or those left from a roast. Put them in water and boil them for several hours with some celery, onion, carrot and other vegetables. It will make delicious soap.'

'John and James Allsop were aged 12 and 17 when they first moved to the town. Now they are its most senior residents. John is 88 and James is 39.'

'The ladies of the Helping Hand Society enjoyed a social swap evening on Friday. They each brought along something that they no longer needed. Many of the ladies were accompanied by their husbands.'

'Mr Harold Starkey said that the neighbourhood had once been quiet and pleasant where children and dogs riding bicycles could play safely in the streets.'

'A bicycle that belonged to a Boy Scout leaning against a wall was damaged in the accident.'

'The bride wore a white gown trimmed with lace and pearls. The bridesmaids' dresses were in a lovely shade of punk.'

' "While on holiday in Kenya we spent one evening at a waterhole where we saw elephants and lions come to drink," said Mrs Harris, adding that they had worn jumpers and brought flasks of hot coffee with them.'

'Colonel Marooney, the bottle-scarred veteran, died at his home last week aged 92.'

'The bride wore a long lace dress that fell all the way to the floor.'

'A package containing drugs was found by a sniffer dog in a suitcase.'

'On Thursday evening the Women's Institute will hold their fortnightly lecture in St Mary's Hall. The topic will be 'Country Life' and Mrs Wills will show slides of some beautiful wild pants.'

'On several occasions Mr Borodin tried to get the 200-year-old violin back, but Miss Framm claimed that the violin was a gift to her with no strings attached.'

'British Rail are looking at the idea of improving the service between London and Luton by making more trains stop at Luton.'

'After complaints that elderly people found it difficult to climb the hill, the council agreed to put a seat at the top.'

'Stolen from a house in Oakleaf Road last Thursday morning were two fur goats and a television set.'

'The route taken by the Princess of Wales was lined with clapping, cheering crows.'

'Mr Hawkins planned to build the bungalow himself using books borrowed from the town library.'

'The robber dropped the hi-fi and began to run, but the police soon caught up with him. It was discovered that he had a record.'

'Last night she discovered the cat dead in her garden and curried its body indoors.'

'The prime minister looked tired after yesterday's meeting and friends say that she is suffering from metal fatigue.'

'Coal and cake have been minced in Wales for hundreds of years, but the closure of the pit may put an end to that.'

'According to the study, Southport is a town with an increasing population of over-65s. This could cause grave problems.'

'During the lecture on how to make home movies the audience saw a demonstration of a child eating a doughnut, a parrot in a cage and a man playing football.'

'Mr and Mrs David Collins wish to announce the birth of their daughter William Thomas on 17 July 1986.'

'Mr Davidson writes a personal reply to all the anonymous letters he receives.'

'We want to produce dancers who at 16 can walk into the Royal Ballet School and stand on their own two feet.'

'The ladies of St Martin's Church have discarded clothing of all kinds.'

'Mr Dennis Harris, playing solo trumpet in the Bedford Band, was awarded the medal for the best trombone player. Brian Franks received the medal for best burglar.'

'Eleven tents were pitched and nearly twenty youngsters converged on the camping sight. Wood was chopped and a general purpose fire lit under Mr Tom Watson, and soon the drizzly atmosphere was flavoured with the scent of wholesome sizzling.'

'The doctor has compiled a list of poisons and dangerous drugs which children can drink in their own homes.'

'The Miners' Union agreed to hold a ballet at the 24 pits before pressing the case.'

'FIRE STATION. It will be much easier to find the Fire Station in future as on Wednesday last a sign reading 'Fire Station' was erected outside the station.'

'A tornado swept through the city last night, doing damage to humerous buildings.'

'The police have issued a photofit picture of the burglar who they describe as a man in his thirties wearing a bear.'

'Princess Alexandra today pressed a button and unveiled a plague to mark the opening of the new reservoir.'

'Miss Logan took over the Weight Watchers Class last week and is concentrating on physical phatness exercises.'

'The Women's Institute annual fancy dress party was held last week. The ladies were asked to come dressed like tramps, which was easy for most of them.'

'The Ladies of the Mothers' Union threw themselves into the tea, which proved a great attraction.'

'St Joseph's School Christmas party was hell yesterday.'

'The Prime Minister made her point by thumping the table with her fish.'

'The ban on children at the local maternity unit has been lifted.'

'The service was held at 11.00 a.m. by the Reverend Nicholas Evans. His sermon was on the subject "The Evil member of the Church". The choir sang the anthem. "Who Can it Be?" '

'There will be a free classical music concert held in the Community Hall on Saturday evening at 7 p.m. Admission £1.00.'

'The new hospital extension will enable patients to be prepared and served in a way that has not been possible before.'

'Peter Wood of Grimsby was fined £25 pounds for using a colour television without a silencer.'

'When the mobile clinic arrived more than fifty children took advantage of it and were examined for tuberculosis and other diseases which the clinic offered free.'

'Roy Rogers, the famous singing cowboy and film star, was described as being in a "stable condition" after an operation last week.'

'Cricket News. The Sussex team won the toss and chose to bath first.'

'The Queen named the ship as she slid gently into the water.'

'As the Queen and Duke of Edinburgh entered the room the trumpeters played a funfair composed specially for the occasion.'

'Visitors to the cemetery are asked not to pick flowers from any of the graves except their own.'

'Mrs Richards recently bought a cow and now she can supply the whole neighbourhood with milk, butter and eggs.'

'The toilets on Platform 9 at Liverpool Street Station are out of order but travellers can use platforms 4, 11 and 16.'

'James Porter returns to work this week after six weeks off due to leg and thingh injuries.'

'This year marks the thirtieth anniversary of the death of the film director Eisenstein, as well as the eighteenth anniversary of his birth.'

'A youth who stole £500 worth of goods from a school was fined £40 at Edinburgh Sheriff Court. He stole two Language Masters, a number of musical instruments and other items.'

'At the village concert Mr Groves, a local dairy farmer, did one of his comic churns.'

'The Reverend John Brown attended a coffee morning at St James's Church last Saturday morning and stole £22.'

'A series of strikes at the local hospital has caused a lot of ill feeling among patients and staff.'

'Mr Nigel Wallis dined at his home in King's Lynn on Thursday. The funeral will be held tomorrow at 2 p.m.'

'June was the hottest month on record. There were only three days without sin all month.'

'GARDENING TIPS: it's time to tie all your pants up with garden twine to protect them from the wind.'

'There will be a guided walk around the town on Sunday afternoon, but if it rains in the afternoon the walk will be held in the morning.'

'There was a good turn-out at the bawling green on Saturday.'

'Thieves stole more than 200 loaves of bread from an empty delivery van this morning.'

'On Sunday the band will be playing in the park. The seats around the bandstand are for the use of ladies. Gentleman should make use of them only after the former are seated.'

'Before Miss Pollard concluded the concert with her rendition of *At the End of a Perfect Day* she was prevented with a large bouquet of carnations from the mayoress.'

'It is small wonder that morale is low. Dentists inadequately paid for their work are said to be pulling out in droves.'

'Len Lyon, leader of the union, has denied throwing a Spaniard in the works.'

The Dotty Dictionary

The English language is full of words that have more than one meaning or words that look just like each other but mean totally different things. So if you've ever had any trouble defining words you'll appreciate this dotty dictionary!

ABUNDANCE A disco in a baker's shop.
ACCORD A fat piece of string.
ACORN Something caused by wearing tight shoes.
ADORE The entrance to a room.
ARCHAEOLOGIST A man whose career is in ruins.
BACHELOR A man who never Mrs anyone.
BACTERIA The back door of a cafeteria.
BANKS Where the river keeps its money.
BIGAMIST A person who makes the same mistake twice.

BIRD HOUSE Home tweet home.

BORE A person who has nothing to say but says it anyway.

BUOYANT A male insect.

CALVES Two animals that follow your footsteps.

CANNIBAL A person who is fed up with people.

CARTOON A song for singing in a car.

CLOAK The sound made by a Chinese Frog.

COCONUT Someone who is crazy about drinking cocoa.

DEAD RINGER A disconnected telephone.

DEFEAT What you walk on.

DENIAL A famous Egyptian river.

DISEASE The parts of the world covered in water.

DIVINE Where grapes grow.

ECHO Something that will always talk to you.

ECLIPSE What a gardener does with his hedge.

ELEPHANT Shy animals who always wear trunks – even in the bath.

ENGINEERS What an engine hears with.

EXPLAIN Eggs without bacon.

EXTINCT A dead skunk.

FATTIE A thin person who has gone to waist.

FIREPROOF The boss's relatives.

FISSION What scientists eat with chips.
FLEA An insect that has gone to the dogs.
FOUL LANGUAGE Rude chickens.
GALLOWS Where no noose is good noose.

GAOL Free accommodation.
GIRAFFE The highest form of animal life.
GOLDFISH A wet pet.
GOOD MANNERS The noise you don't make when
    you slurp your soup.
GOOSE A bird that grows down as it grows up.
GUILLOTINE Something that gives you a pain in
    the neck.
HALO What two angels say when they greet each
    other.
HARP A nude piano.
HATCHET What a chicken does with an egg.
HUMPHREY An ideal name for a camel without
    any humps.

ICE CREAM Yell at the top of your voice.
ILLEGAL A sick bird.
INCREASES A shirt that has been under your bed
    for a week.

INFORMATION How the Red Devils fly.

INTENSE How Girl Guides sleep on holiday.

ITCH What happens to your back when your hands are full.

JARGON A missing jam container.

JITTERBUG A nervous insect.

JOAN OF ARC Noah's wife.

JUMP The last word in aeroplanes.

JUNK Something you hoard for years and then throw out the day before it comes in useful.

KANGAROO A pogo stick with a pouch.

KIDNAP What a baby has after lunch.

KING COLE The monarch who invented cole slaw.

KNOB Something to adore.

LAP Something you lose every time you stand up.

LAUNCH Astronaut's midday meal.

LAWSUIT What policemen wear.

LEOPARD An animal that's easy to spot.

LIFT ATTENDANT A person who has his ups and downs.

LISP When you call a spade a thpade.

LUNATIC A clock that lives on the moon.

MARKET What teachers do to exams.

MEATBALL A butchers' dance.
MELANCHOLY The favourite fruit of collie dogs.
MINIMUM A small mother.

MOONBEAMS What keeps the moon up.
MOUSTACHE A soup strainer.
MUMBO JUMBO A confused elephant.

NIGHTINGALE A windy evening.

NIGHTMARE A horse who likes to stay out late.

NITRATE The opposite of day rate.

NORMALISE Excellent vision.

OBOE An ill wind instrument that blows no one any good.

OHM The place where you live.

OLD-TIMER A grandfather clock.

OPERA A play with music in which people sing and then die.

ORANGE A fruit with a lot of appeal.

OUCH Sound made by two hedgehogs kissing.

OUT-OF-BOUNDS An exhausted kangaroo.

PARADOX Two doctors.

PASTEURISE Beyond what you can see.

PENGUIN A bird who wears a dinner jacket in bed.

PERFUME A best-smeller.

PIGGY BANK The place where pigs keep their money.

PLANET What you should do before you go on a journey.

PRINTER A man of letters.

QUACK A doctor who treats ducks.

QUARTZ Four to the gallon.

RAISIN A worried grape.

REFUSE What you do when the lightbulbs blow.

RELIEF What trees do each spring.

RESEARCH Look for something again.

RHUBARB Celery with high blood pressure.

ROBIN A bird thief.

ROCKET The only way to get baby astronauts to sleep.

SAGO The way to start a pudding race.

SANDWICH An attempt to make both ends meet.

SEASICKNESS What doctors do all day.

SHOEHORN A musical instrument that plays footnotes.

SLEEPING BAG A nap sack.

SOOT What a chimney sweep wears.

SOURPUSS A cat that swallowed a lemon.

TAXI DRIVER A man who makes a living by driving people round the bend.

TELEVISION A watching machine.

TERRIBLE Anything you can rip easily.

TORTOISE What the teacher did.

TREASON The male offspring of a tree.

TRIFLE A dessert that can shoot.

TURTLE A lizard with a mobile home.

UNAWARE What you put on first thing every morning.

UNDERCOVER POLICEMAN A policeman in bed.

UNIT Term of abuse.

UNIVERSITY A city in space.

URCHIN The lower parts of a person's face.

URGENT A woman's boyfriend.

VESTRY A room in a church where vests are kept.

VICIOUS CIRCLE A round geometrical figure with a nasty temper.

VINE A weak plant that cannot support itself.

VIOLIN A nasty pub.

VOLCANO A mountain that's blown its top.

WATER Thirst aid.

WATERMELON A fruit that you can eat, drink and wash your face in at the same time.

WED The colour of marriage.

WISECRACKER Clever crispbread.

WITCHCRAFT A flying broomstick.

X What chickens lay.

X-RAY Belly-vision.

YANK An American dentist.

YEAR What you hear with.

ZEBRA A horse wearing pyjamas.

ZINC Where you do the washing-up.

ZUB The noise made by a bee flying backwards.

Headline Howlers

A mistake in a headline can make even the most boring news worth reading! Misprints, misunderstandings and major mistakes — you'll find them all here.

MAN FOUND WITH POLICEMAN IN BOOT

MAN DIED AFTER ATTEMPTING TO COMMIT SUICIDE

POLICE ACT IN STOLEN BOOK CASE

CHICKEN THIEF NOT GUILTY: Judge blames police for wild goose chase.

ELECTRICITY BILLS CAUSE NEW SHOCKS

BACHELORS PREFER BEAUTY TO BRAINS IN THEIR WIVES

BOY RECOVERS AFTER FATAL CAR CRASH

POLICEMAN FOUND DRUNK IN TELEPHONE BOX

CHANNEL SWIM ATTEMPT: Boston girl arrives in Liverpool

SENIOR CITIZENS JUMBLE SALE: LOTS OF ANTIQUES

VICARS' STRIKE: HELL TO PAY, SAYS BISHOP

MORE MEN MARRIED THAN WOMEN

HEN-PECKED HUSBAND COOKED FOR FORTY YEARS

PRINCE TOASTS PRESIDENT

PRISONERS ESCAPE AFTER EXECUTION

HOTEL BURNS DOWN: 200 GUESTS ESCAPE HALF-GLAD

MAN CRITICAL AFTER BUS REVERSES INTO HIM

GASMEN GRILLED BY ANGRY VILLAGERS

DETECTIVES SEIZE TWO WOMENS PIES

VIOLENCE – JUDGES HIT OUT

PUPILS MARCH OVER NEW TEACHERS

MOVIE STAR FOUND DAD IN BATH

VOLUNTARY WORKERS FIGHT FOR HIGHER PAY

20 YEAR FRIENDSHIP ENDS AT ALTAR

PEACE OR WAR DEEMED NEAR

PUBLIC HEALTH HAZARD: COMMITTEE TO SIT ON RATS

COUNCIL 'DIGGING OWN GRAVE': Smaller bodies urged

WOMAN CLINGS TO BUOY FOR NINE HOURS

AUTHOR BLAMES PRINTER FOR BAD SPEELING

ALL CISTERNS GO FOR NEW SEWAGE FARM

BURGLAR FRACTURES VICTIM'S SKULL BUT FINDS NOTHING IN IT

POLICEMAN ACCUSED OF ACCEPTING BRIDE

GREAT SERVICE TO EDUCATION: Local headmaster resigns

SLAUGHTERHOUSE STAFF TO BE CUT IN HALF

THREE BATTERED IN FISH SHOP – MAN GAOLED FOR ASSAULT

GROCER DREADED BECOMING CABBAGE

FOOD PRICES RISE: Grocers say they will not hit housewives

MAN DENIES COMMITTING SUICIDE

RSPCA WILL ARRANGE PAINLESS END FOR OWNERS OF BIRDS: Fears of parrot disease

NEW YORK BANS BOXING AFTER DEATH

MAYORESS RECEIVES SILVER BRUSH AND BOMB SET

COUNCILLORS DISCUSS RUBBISH

STUDENTS MARCH OVER FOREIGN TOURISTS

ANGRY BULL INJURES FARMER WITH AXE

LUCKY MAN SEES FRIENDS DIE

NEW POISON THREAT AS MINISTER HEADS FOR BEACHES

SOUFFLE AT SUPERMARKET: Fighting breaks out over wrong change

AMERICAN CHICKENS LAY 800 EGGS A MINUTE

HEADLESS, HANDLESS AND FOOTLESS BODY FOUND: POLICE SUSPECT FOUL PLAY

SINGING THREAT FOR PENSIONERS: Famous singer gives free concert

DEAD POLICEMAN IN THE FORCE FOR 12 YEARS

BRIDE OF SIX MOUTHS SUES HUSBAND FOR DIVORCE

JAPANESE TO SCRUB TURKISH BATHS

BANANA OPENS PARLIAMENT: Zimbabwe news

COUNCIL DECIDES TO MAKE SAFE DANGER SPOTS

MAN IN RIVER HAD A DRINK PROBLEM

PRESS MEN GATHER TO SEE ROYALS HUNG AT WINDSOR: New portraits on show at castle

And now the late News . . .

Short-sighted racing driver Mike Brown today explained why he took 32 pit-stops during the British grand prix. The first was to refuel, the other 31 were to ask the way.

The Yorkshire sheepdog trials were held today. Three dogs, Spot, Shep and Lady, were found guilty.

Members of a Devon gardening club have announced that in future they'll be using cows to cut the grass for them. They call them 'lawn moo-ers'.

Here is some advice for holidaymakers. If someone collapses on the beach this summer, make sure that you turn them over so that they get an even tan.

A woman who dreamt that she had eaten a huge marshmallow during the night was rushed to hospital when her husband realized that her pillow had disappeared.

A punk rock group gave a concert in Ipswich last night and threw a stick of dynamite into the audience. It brought the house down.

A woman from Portsmouth has bought herself 50 kilos of steel wool and a large set of knitting needles. She intends to knit herself an electric cooker.

The body of a man was discovered in a burnt-out henhouse on Saturday. Police do not suspect foul play.

Arthur Mozart, the famous composer, has announced that after spending a week stuck in his bath he will in the future write soap operas.

Police are looking for thieves who broke into a shop and stole packs of playing cards. A spokesman said they intend to catch them at their own game.

A man who came home from work last Monday and found a gorilla sleeping in his bed has explained how he coped with the situation. He went and slept in the other room.

The government has announced that from tomorrow all cars must drive on the right. If the experiment is successful, lorries and buses will join in the following day.

Two prisoners have escaped from the gaol. One of them is seven foot tall and the other is just four feet six. Police are searching high and low for them.

News has come in from America that Brad Brown the famous plastic surgeon has died. He sat on a radiator, melted and made a complete pool of himself.

MP Cyril Smith has been dropped from his local tug-o-war team because he was not pulling his own weight.

A new scissors shop opened in Sunderland today. The owners say that it's a cut above the rest.

Trains from Euston station were running 5 minutes late yesterday. British Rail apologized and said that today they are running normally again — 10 minutes late.

Anyone who would like to go on a cruise on the Norfolk Broads with Russell Grant and Cyril Smith should apply for tickets immediately because space is very limited.

Police in Leicester are hunting for a tabby tom cat that has been missing for a week. It is described as mainly brown, blind in one eye, with one ear missing, a bad limp and only a stump of tail. It answers to the name Lucky.

The guard at Buckingham Palace has just been changed and says he feels much better in his clean nappy.

Two men who were arrested at Covent Garden for stealing fruit are reported to have had their Legal Aid application refused. They've been told to make do with Lemon Aid instead.

A Sealink ferry captain today announced that he'd found a cure for seasickness — a very tight collar.

The annual general meeting of the Fortune-Tellers' Association has had to be cancelled due to unforseen circumstances.

A survey shows that some people are being over-charged for funerals costs. 'People are being taken for a ride by funeral directors,' said a spokesman.

Finally, doctors attending a medical conference have agreed that there's really only one cure for insomnia and that's a good night's sleep.

22   18